Contents

Acknowledgments

"But thanks be to God, who always leads us in triumphal procession in Christ and through us spreads everywhere the fragrance of the knowledge of him" (2 Corinthians 2:14 NIV).

I want to express my gratitude to God for placing in my heart the desire to write this book. I leaned on Him every step of the way, just like I had to do through my illness. He is faithful in every circumstance.

Thanks to my sweet husband, Tim, for his many "reads" of rewrites as I endeavored to share my heart. I thank Tim, also, for believing in me and encouraging me to "just start."

Thanks to my sons, Andy and Matt, who graciously shared their skills in technology to assist me in many ways.

Thanks to my sister, Nancy, who listened many times over the phone as I shared something I had just written to get her feedback.

Thanks to the many that encouraged me to finish my book after hearing me tell my story.

Introduction

Today I walk in thanksgiving and perpetual amazement at what God has done for me. Each day is a gift and a reminder of what I can do now that I could not do for such a long time. The little things that I used to take for granted now cause my heart to leap. Being able to walk with balance and ease – a miracle. Being able to sleep through the night without pain, fear and anxiety – a blessing. Being able to take care of my home, go to the grocery store, take evening walks with my husband, cook dinner, load the dishwasher, pull weeds in the flower beds – all gifts. Being able to run and play with my grandchildren – priceless. Having the strength to talk on the phone, play the piano, hold and read my Bible, all gifts that I pray I will never take for granted.

Most of us have common abilities that we just don't recognize as gifts until they're gone. My story is one of miraculous healing with an equally significant story of God's faithfulness and provision during the long storm.

My neighbor asked me one day, "How do I get to where you are without going through what you've been through?" Very good question I thought. So I considered that question, prayed about what God would have me share, and began a book about my journey.

Part One tells the story of my illness and miraculous healing.

Part Two conveys personal experiences and application of principles to help the reader walk toward a more complete trust in and dependence upon a loving Heavenly

Father. I learned that trust and dependence on Him is a must for true peace, happiness and health.

Come on the journey with me and share in the marvelous truths of His healing for our whole being, body, soul, mind, and spirit.

Part One

My Story

Chapter One

The First Domino Falls

"It's long-term and extensive. I don't want to tell you everything, now. Let's get the pain under control and get you through your son's wedding. Be careful not to yawn or laugh. You can take your appliance out for the wedding pictures only."

Two weeks later...

"It's permanent. I sent your x-rays to a specialist who deals with TMJ entirely and he confirmed my diagnosis. You'll have to wear your appliance 24/7 except when you brush your teeth."

"Will I be able to eat?!!!!"

"You'll eat again, but different. You'll learn to mash your food first and just swallow bigger pieces."

"But, my teeth don't come together."

"Bebe, your teeth will never come together again. You're going to need a good chiropractor because everything will go out of alignment. Since your jaw is out of alignment you will need adjustments on your neck, your shoulders, your back, your hips, everything. I am going to make a new appliance for you – it will be better. They're expensive but they usually last up to four years."

Dazed, I silently walked out of the office into the lobby. I had contacted several dentists for help and this was the only one who was willing to do something. Others just referred me back to the original dentist. As shock turned into grief, guttural sobs preceded tears. Oblivious to passers in the parking lot, I entered my car and drove home. I cried out to God, but I didn't even know what to say. My chest felt heavy and empty at the same time. It was as if I couldn't breathe. I felt totally without hope. There was no solution, no fix.

I walked into the house and began to tell my husband what I had learned. As I spoke, all the emotion gushed out in spite of my efforts. How could this be? Three months ago I was fine.

Some background: At the recommendation of my father, I had gone to a new dentist to have my teeth cleaned. The dentist suggested that I needed work done on several teeth. The office administrator met with me to discuss the procedure and related costs; payment was to be made upfront so as to receive a reduction in price. At the next visit a mold was taken of my jaw, old fillings and crowns removed, and temporary crowns were made and affixed.

The process had been long and involved and required numerous injections to deaden my mouth. When I got home my husband said I looked as if I had had a stroke because my face was so paralyzed from the numbing shots. As soon as the medication wore off I started having discomfort and tension in my jaw. The fit was wrong and I informed the dentist's office of the pain I was experiencing. They assured me that with the permanent crowns everything would be better.

Several weeks later, still in constant pain, the temporary work was replaced with permanent crowns. It was a grueling long procedure because my jaw was already so stressed. I had explained to the dentist that now when I ate, my jaw would completely get off track. When this would happen, I would be unable to close my mouth until I manipulated my jaw back into position with my hands. It was very painful. This actually happened while he was working on me. He was working in my mouth with my head completely back and tilted down toward the floor. I learned later that this position places your jaw in a very vulnerable position while making the dentist's job easier. His eyes widened and he watched as I manipulated my jaw back into position. He quietly continued with the procedure. I had to ask to rest my jaw several times; it took hours.

The dentist lost his grasp on one of the new crowns while holding it in my mouth with my head back and tilted. Fortunately, even though my mouth was so numb, my tongue reacted and stopped the crown from going down my throat. His comment, "Good save."

There was no improvement. I continued to inform the dentist of the difficulties I was experiencing. A week or two later I called and asked for a muscle relaxant for my jaw. It had been recommended by another doctor that a muscle relaxant might help. Instead the dentist prescribed a pain medication which did not help at all.

Improper fitting had caused misalignment resulting in unrelenting pain. The culpable dentist continued to ignore and deny my problems for many weeks. Finally my jaw muscles let go as in a rubber band strained to the point of snapping. It was explained to me that this muscle breakdown had left both mandibular condyles (jaw joints) permanently out of position. The new dentist who was trying to help me said surgery was the only way to fix the problem but she highly advised against it. I researched and found that it was extremely risky surgery with no guarantee of outcome. Many times this type of jaw surgery resulted in more pain and complete physical impairment.

An innocuous trip to the dentist, poor dentistry, professional indifference to my pain combined with what x-rays revealed to be a very old injury had resulted in a permanent change to life as I had known it.

This was only the tip of the iceberg. My husband and I had experienced one of the most financially stressful years of our thirty-one wonderful years together. However, there were blessings mixed in with our troubles; our oldest son had graduated from college and had a great job and a very special girl (whom he later married); our youngest was finishing his last year of college and had just married his precious childhood sweetheart. But the degree of pain and stress we suddenly shared with this new revelation attempted to swallow us up.

I knew God was faithful. I knew things could be a lot worse. But I was angry. I was angry that this could happen. I was angry that this dentist could be so inept. I was angry that he denied any responsibility; that he didn't even seem to care. I learned about six months later from a qualified seasoned dentist that all of this could have been avoided if the original dentist had just fixed his mistake. My husband was angry that someone had done this to me, and despaired that he could do nothing to help. I was struggling to speak clearly with the new appliance, and continued to be unable to eat or sleep with the intense pain. Anxiety and fear overwhelmed me.

As shallow as it seems, I saddened at the thought of never being able to eat a hamburger again, or munch on pretzels or carrots. I personally get a lot of pleasure from eating good food. And, I enjoy cooking! Now, I was spending a great deal of time just trying to get basic nutrients into my body. Several times a day I was processing food in the blender so I could drink it or eat it with a spoon.

We asked our Sunday school class to pray for me and one of the members told me about a friend of his who specialized in treating people with TMJ. We set up an appointment with him but would have to wait several weeks.

An amazing thing happened. God began to work in my heart and mind. He helped me recognize with a new certainty that whatever happened, it would be temporary. Our life here is only a temporary condition. We were made to spend eternity with God in new, imperishable bodies. He gave me an unexplainable peace that whatever happened He would be with me. He hadn't made any of the bad things happen, but He had allowed them for some reason and He would be faithful to work His purposes in it, purposes for my good and His glory. He proved His love for me 2,000 years ago on the cross and He had proved His faithfulness to me over and over again through the years.

Chapter Two

Hope and Forgiveness

Tim and I went to the new specialist eager to hear his diagnosis. Would he confirm the conclusions of two others? Was God going to heal me? Did this doctor have other information?

After extensive testing he sat down with my husband and me, confirmed my condition and said, "If you decide to be treated by me, here's the plan. I will make a new orthotic appliance for stabilizing your upper jaw. You will wear this 24/7 except when you eat or brush your teeth." I jumped in at this point and had him repeat his statement.

"I'll eat?"

"Yes, you'll eat."

"With my teeth?"

"Yes, with your teeth. You will retrain your brain to develop and use new strands of muscles and tendons. You will no longer chew in a circular motion or back and forth, but will learn how to chew in a straight up-and-down fashion. You will stay on soft foods and gradually add more regular foods as you are able. The appliance will help pull away old tendons and muscles and you will have exercises and stretches to help build and strengthen new ones. In about six months, if your jaw is stabilized, we will gradually begin to try weaning you from daytime use of your appliance, but you will always have to wear it at night and during times of stress."

"Will there be things I can't eat?"

"You won't be able to eat ice or unpopped kernels of corn at the bottom of the bag."

"I'll eat popcorn?!!!"

"Yes."

Hope! A new understanding of hope! Many people live as if they have no hope. We are promised that there will be trials and struggles, but when my soul is downcast I will remember, *"Put your hope in God"* (Psalm 42:5 NIV). God has *"plans to give you hope and a future"* (Jeremiah 29:11 NIV). I have a new desire to share that hope. In the *New Spirit Filled Life Bible*, the word hope is defined in the "Word Wealth" section following 1 Thessalonians 1:3 as a "confident expectation based on solid certainty." Read that again, "a confident expectation based on solid certainty." Isn't that amazing? Through the next seven years that kind of hope would be built in my mind and heart.

. . . .

I fought the anger that I felt toward the dentist who caused my problems. I refused to share or smear his name; I believed that he and his assistants had made a series of combined errors in judgment and procedure, but not as a result of intended harm. My husband and I did go to see him and ask him to help make things right. He denied any wrongdoing. In subsequent newsletters the dentist was now addressing problems with TMJ so I felt he was aware of his mistakes and precautions he should take. I did speak with an attorney about seeking compensation for the expenses ahead of me; however, I was advised by a specialist from whom he sought counsel that because I was "alive and walking" damages would be too small for a law firm to want to take the case. Insurance does not cover treatments for TMJ. There is more, but let's move on.

I chose to forgive, but it took time. I made myself pray for the dentist and asked God to teach him and to bless him. And I asked the Lord to keep me from unforgiveness and bitterness. Again, it was a process. Sometimes we have to choose to forgive the same person for the same thing every day. But we have been given the gift of choice. When we choose not to forgive, we choose to carry the weight of unforgiveness; it is very heavy and costly. Have you ever forgiven someone only to have that same issue pop into your mind months later, and with a vengeance? Well, the enemy will try to pull up old wounds, won't he? But we have the wisdom of God's word; *"And be ye kind one to another, tenderhearted, forgiving one another even as God for Christ's sake hath forgiven you"* (Ephesians 4:32 KJV). As God's child, God has forgiven me of all my sin because of Christ's sacrifice. However, He doesn't ask me to forgive in my own strength. I couldn't. But, *"I can do all things through Christ who strengthens me"* (Philippians 4:13 NKJV). His Spirit is at work in us to make us mighty by His power.

Today, when I see the dentist's name or picture in an advertisement, I choose to pray for him and his family. I pray first for their salvation. I pray that this man will be a godly husband and father, that the Lord will accomplish every purpose He has designed for his life, and that he may live to the praise of God's glory. I also pray that he will never cause another serious injury to a patient. It is a choice I make, but I give God all the glory for enabling me to forgive this wrong and to pray for this man's well-being.

Chapter Three

More Dominoes Fall

I gradually learned to chew a new way and after many months my new jaw muscles were becoming stronger. The orthotic appliance was helping with the pain in my jaw, but I continued to alternate ice and heat and perform the prescribed jaw exercises several times a day to help with the tension. I still had to wear the appliance most of the time except when eating or brushing my teeth and it was difficult to speak so people could understand me. My husband had a number of chuckles at my attempts to pronounce certain words. Sleep was very difficult and I continued to lose weight. The jaw pain, insomnia, constant back and neck problems, worry and stress were taking their toll on my body.

Because of everything that was happening to my body, my hair was falling out, quickly. Somehow, that was almost worse than the constant pain. I felt as if I were losing my femininity. When most of my hair was gone and I was too embarrassed to go out in public, my husband jumped in to the rescue. "Bebe, I saw a wig salon close to the hospital. Let's go and find you a wig." So my sweet husband took me shopping! I had short light brown hair with subtle touches of gray; of course not much was left. The first wig the clerk put on my head was long, straight, jet-black hair. I tried to explain to her what my hair had looked like, but then she brought out a red bob. If I had called first, they probably would have told me to bring a picture of what I looked like before. My husband just smiled and went browsing for the right look. He came back with the cutest, perkiest short wig; it even had a few little highlighted spikes on top, and the color was perfect. It made me feel beautiful.

Because of our financial situation and no insurance for my jaw treatments, I had been reluctant about seeking medical help for my other physical problems. About a year into this ordeal, I finally went to see a doctor who discovered that most of my hormones had completely shut down. She said my body was in survival mode, just doing what it had to do. She was very helpful, prescribed bio-identical hormones and thyroid and I began to improve, but she moved away. That started me on a roller coaster with other doctors, some untrained in what they were attempting, some trained but confused by my symptoms and even one doctor relying again and again on what we learned later to be compromised lab results.

We had a number of other situations pop up during the same time period. My husband and I worked together at his business. Just prior to my jaw injury, we had closed our outside offices to work out of our home in order to save money. We poured everything into the company to try to keep our business afloat, including forgoing our salaries for two years thus depleting our personal savings and retirement. Finally, my husband made the decision to close his company, a business that he worked to build for over 25 years. We were able to pay all the bills owed to vendors, finish the projects he was building, and close the company in the black; we were grateful for that. Tim had a wealth of experience and a great reputation and gratefully was able to go to work for a company based on the same principles of business he had followed all those years. However, the previous months had taken a terrible toll on my husband. He watched his dream fade away and I watched a broken man lose his confident stride.

In the midst of all this, my ninety-one year old father was sued, by what should have been a frivolous law suit, but somehow the case was taken forward and I was responsible for helping him. He was a retired minister who had given his life as a dedicated pastor. He was probably known most for his faithful hospital ministry. He still lived on his own and was doing well for his age, but required a lot of help. My brother came by to have an early cup of coffee with our dad whenever possible. My sister helped a lot in the evenings and weekends, but she, too, had to work so I took him to his doctor appointments, sharing trips to the store and other errands, and helping him with some of his meals. One of his favorite things to do was to go out to eat.

I found an attorney and we proceeded to spend a lot of Daddy's money fighting the lawsuit. The worry and extensive time spent dealing with this case took a large toll on me and my dad. Toward the end of the case our attorney passed away suddenly and we had to pick up from there with another attorney. The truth did come out in the end but after a long battle and a lot of expense that we were unable to recover.

But it was finally over. Once again I had to let it go, choose to forgive, and move forward. But my movements were becoming more and more labored as my body, mind, and emotions became more and more frayed. Because of the added stress, Daddy had suffered a number of mini-strokes. He was becoming less competent and more easily agitated and anxious. He spoke some things in his frustration that were very hurtful and very hard to handle. He was becoming more and more demanding and in retrospect I believe he was becoming fearful as his abilities diminished. I began to carry these things deep in my heart along with other unresolved issues, those things we stuff down inside and think we've resolved, forgiven, or forgotten.

Chapter Four

The Beat Goes On and on and on

The next couple of years were like a downhill roller-coaster. There were times when I was feeling a little stronger and times when the fatigue and weakness were overwhelming, but I kept marching on. There were things that just had to be done and I felt I had to do them. I even wrote and taught a Bible study course, and though it was good to be back teaching, I was pushing too hard. What I came to understand later was even when I was doing a little better physically, I had no reserve, and so I would quickly be back where I started – at the end of myself.

Because I was so drained, I began to resent some of the responsibilities of caring for Daddy; I felt trapped. He seemed unable to understand what I was going through physically and he had become very demanding in his expectations. My steps had become so short and labored and he was so bent over that I laughed at our appearance together. Daddy had almost 40 years on me but you couldn't tell it by my pace. Disappointments seemed to multiply; weariness of heart became the norm. The smallest of tasks loomed monumental. I got behind in everything. Actually I hadn't been able to keep up for a long time, but it became burdensome. I added stress to stress and worry to worry.

Often it was actually difficult for me to put one foot in front of the other and I became very hypoglycemic. My speech would begin to slur and I would become incredibly sleepy and unable to carry on a conversation. I would find a place to lie down, or if in a restaurant I would have to lay my head on the table. I couldn't reason and I would refuse Tim's suggestion that I drink some orange juice until he would just insist. That would help almost immediately. Oddly enough, another thing that would bring me out of that kind of slump was a big thick juicy hamburger, even just the meat. (Yes, by now I could remove one of the sides of the bun and carefully chew the meat and bread.) One doctor suggested I drink protein drinks and so I consumed two to three protein drinks each day, a portion between each meal, but I continued to lose strength and weight. (Years later a naturopathic doctor explained that protein transports the glucose.)

An endocrinologist had me go through a glucose test and everything tested fine. However, about 15 minutes after leaving the testing lab I experienced the "crash" that had become so familiar. The doctor wasn't interested in what happened when I left, he just read the numbers on the test and said my blood glucose was fine. For years I had been very careful to eat the right foods, avoid sugar, and take my hormones and supplements faithfully. However, one doctor checked my blood for nutrient absorption and found me to be very deficient in most areas of nutrition in spite of a healthy diet and the volumes of quality supplements I was taking.

One evening as Tim and I prepared for bed, Daddy called; he had fallen and broken his hip. It took him forty-five minutes to pull himself to the phone. We called 911 as we rushed to his home. The next six weeks were devastating. The surgeon warned us that there was the possibility that he would never be the same after surgery because of his age. He had just celebrated his ninety-fifth birthday, but we were used to a man who just seemed to keep on going, no matter what. He had learned to swim in his fifties and water ski in his sixties. Before he had open heart surgery in his late seventies, he loved to perform on trick skis and stand on a wooden chair while skiing on a round wooden platform. He had cared for my mother who suffered from debilitating back pain for over thirty years. After my mother passed away, Daddy moved into a new home closer to us and enjoyed furnishing it "his way". As long as he could drive he kept busy visiting with anybody in his path and even enjoyed delivering groceries to an elderly couple who had been members in his church (they were younger than he). He loved being with people and visited at length with anyone he met. Losing the ability to drive had been devastating to him, but he still had amazing physical and mental drive for a man of his years.

His fall and surgery completely changed everything. He was not recovering well. He was unable to perform the activities they expected of him and he kept telling me something was wrong. He continued to refuse to eat saying he felt like he couldn't, but we kept insisting so his strength could return. They sent him to rehab before he was ready. My husband took me home to get some rest because I didn't have enough strength to even walk, literally. My sister left and met the ambulance at the rehab facility. Daddy refused to eat and the nurse made some derogatory comment about his attitude. My brother came to stay with him and within an hour called saying that Daddy was throwing up large amounts of blood. We got to the rehab center as quickly as possible (my husband practically carrying me in) and then waited and waited for help. I was lying in the bed next to Daddy's. We kept asking them what was taking so long and started being very insistent; they kept telling us that the ambulance was on the way. He was no longer spitting up blood but was very, very weak and only semi-conscious. Several <u>hours</u> later the ambulance arrived and the EMS team worked on him for some time trying to stabilize him. The medical staff at the rehab center had not even started him on intravenous fluids. We were finally on our way; the EMS told us later they didn't think at first he would be able to make it. They had advised us not to return him to the original hospital so we had followed their recommendation and changed locations.

Things did not get better. Daddy was now very incoherent and often hallucinating and agitated. He was not able to get up. His kidneys stopped functioning well and they began treating him with insulin for diabetes, a new development, and at the same time feeding him sugary liquid supplements. Once I was aware of the insulin, I questioned the combination. After working through a maze of personnel, I finally was able to get that rectified. The medical staff looked at Daddy as a ninety-five year old invalid; they didn't know what he was like just a few weeks prior. They had given up on him but we had not.

Daddy had not been around much while we were growing up. He was one of those ministers who had totally dedicated his life to the church, at the expense of his family. His latter years had been to me an opportunity to have the relationship that we never had. It didn't exactly turn out that way, but I felt an overwhelming responsibility to help my dad. Because I was his legal representative, it fell on me to be with him most every day. My sister and brother would alternate evenings and my brother stayed with him through many nights. Invariably, if I would leave for a time during the day to get some rest at home, one of the floor nurses would call me and tell me to come right back because I needed to sign some form or make some kind of decision. I would leave the hospital in the evening and just cry all the way home from emotional and physical exhaustion.

We needed help and the Lord led us to two "angels" who worked full-time in the hospital but also would alternate and come on their off times to help with Daddy. They were two of the sweetest people I've ever known, and Daddy loved them.

After several more weeks with no improvement the medical staff had decided to send him home to die. By begging and cajoling the staff doctors with descriptions of Daddy's abilities in recent months and years, I convinced them to give Daddy another shot at rehab. I told Daddy the physical therapists were coming back to see if he could walk and that he had to give it his best shot. He said, "Not today, maybe later." I got in his face and with tight lips and stern eyes emphatically demanded his attention, "Daddy, they're coming back to see if you can walk. You have to walk to be able to qualify for rehab. Your very life depends on what you do! I want you to muster up all your German will-power and do whatever they tell you to do.

Do You Understand Me?" I'm normally very soft spoken and wouldn't have used that tone with my Daddy, but his life was at stake. His eyes were as wide open as I'd ever seen them and he shook his head, yes.

The director of physical therapy came to the door. I went out in the hall with him and pleaded for my daddy's life as I tried to quickly describe his life of strength and determination. At this point Daddy had put on over forty pounds of fluids and had been in the hospital, totally inactive, for over a month so any effort was extremely difficult. Just for his mind to be lucid for more than a few moments was miraculous at this point. But, my daddy did it! They had him stand for about a minute and then asked him to walk. His eyes were focused on me the whole time and he walked – about six feet. He looked at me for approval and I smiled and exclaimed, "Good job, Daddy!" He collapsed in their arms. They were astounded that he walked so far and they approved rehab – his last hope.

They moved him the next day to a rehab facility next door to the hospital. Our sweet angels went with us to help when they were able. My brother bought him some new clothes as he was unable to fit in anything he owned. We really liked the staff at the rehab facility and they went over the plans for his rehabilitation and recovery. My sister was with him for his first therapy session. She said he really struggled to comply with their requests, but because he was so weak he just couldn't. The staff wanted him out of bed so he slumped in his wheelchair, his body draped over the armrest. He was so confused and asked me when he had gotten so heavy. He had always taken pride in being very fit and trim. Once in his forties, as pastor, he attended a youth camp. Some of the teenagers from our church were taking turns climbing a rope; Daddy muscled up the rope – feet first.

Just a couple of hours after I left the rehab center that evening, the nurse called me to say Daddy had fallen out of bed. We had complained that there were no rails on the bed, but they said it was against the law to put rails up! What kind of law is that? They let me talk with him on the phone and he seemed to be in good spirits, joking about all the pretty girls helping him. However, when I got there the next morning, I couldn't get him to eat or to talk. He seemed really incoherent and nonresponsive and the nurse checked him and called the doctor. They rushed him immediately to the emergency room; he had suffered a major heart attack.

The next few hours were very difficult, but we did have a new staff of doctors in the ER who compassionately and carefully answered our questions and helped us with the decisions we had to make. They admitted Daddy to the hospital while we waited on a hospice representative to come talk with us. Hospice was set up in the hospital as he only had a short time to live. We sat up with him through the night with one of our angels and watched him breathe. He briefly opened his eyes, connected with mine, and I told him, "I love you, Daddy." He mouthed silently, "I love you, too," and shut his eyes for the last time. A couple hours later, he stopped breathing. Our second angel came and joined the first and they prepared my daddy, at their own request. For these weeks they had taken fastidious care of my daddy which is how he lived, a very dignified man.   And now, they prepared him and his bed, with dignity and love.

Chapter Five

An Avalanche

We made the necessary arrangements and pulled through the next few days. God was giving me momentary strength to do what needed to be done, but I was using up reserve that I didn't even possess. My adrenals were shot. There had been momentary hints of recovery through the years, but my body did not have the ability to bounce back again.

I had visited a new endocrinologist who came highly recommended but he just left us with more questions. At this point there were times when I actually could not walk at all. When I did walk my husband said it was like watching the scarecrow in the Wizard of Oz; it felt, to me, like a Raggedy Ann doll. Some evenings I felt I could take a short walk with my husband, but after a very short distance (maybe even one house past our driveway) I would move more and more slowly until my leg muscles would completely stop and I could only slowly force my feet forward microscopic inches at a time. My breathing would become very labored and throaty as I gasped for air, my leg muscles pushing me up on my tiptoes as I clung to my husband to keep from falling over. Before my husband could get me back to the house I would simply collapse. My leg muscles would ache and burn like fire for a couple days, leaving me immobile. When I described the burning to some friends they said it sounded like an intense runner's burn after a marathon, but I hadn't done anything!

Another doctor added cortisol to the mix of hormones and when I didn't improve, he continued to add more and more cortisol. They were treating my adrenals for extreme fatigue. My husband and I kept asking why I couldn't walk and they had no answers. I was not getting better and the expense for all this medical "treatment" was mounting. That was nothing compared to the frustration and anxiety I was experiencing.

While seeking answers for my problems, my husband was set to have skin cancer surgery. He had ignored an area on his forehead for some time. Unfortunately, the doctor, unable to anticipate the spread of the cancer's tentacles, had set the surgery several months out because of scheduling problems. One doctor was to surgically remove the cancer and the following morning, a plastic surgeon was to close the area. If you are unfamiliar with the Mohs treatment, the physician anesthetizes the area and removes a thin layer of tissue surrounding and including the tumor. A dressing is applied and the patient waits while each section of the tissue is examined under a microscope. If the tumor is still present, they repeat this procedure until all areas are free of cancer. I cannot even remember how many times they had to repeat the procedure on Tim, at least four or five. It took most of the day. The bandaged area grew larger each time. Finally, it covered half his forehead. The doctor called us in to speak with us. He said the cancer had developed "long feelers" or roots, I guess, that had extended much farther than he had anticipated. He said he wasn't sure the plastic surgeon would be able to close the entire area. They did not want to do a graft of skin from another area of his body because they said it would look like a big tire patch. The nurse packed his forehead with gauze, told us to apply ice every half hour, take the pain medication as needed, and be at the hospital in the morning.

Our son went with us to the hospital. I was probably more of a liability than an asset at this point, but I wanted and needed to be there. Following the procedure, the surgeon came to speak with me. His eyes were wide and his expression was less than comforting. He explained that the wound was far too large to close. He did the best he could, but Tim would have a large gaping wound that we would need to clean, treat, and cover four times a day for several weeks. Then we were to see him at his office for further instructions. I believe now that the wound should have been closed immediately following the excision before so much swelling had occurred. Recovering in post-op, Tim's blood pressure was so high they did not want to release him. He had been dealing with elevated blood pressure for some time, but was attempting to get it under control himself. Are you realizing this is a man who really doesn't like going to the doctor? His blood pressure came down a little and they agreed to release him, telling him he needed to be checked. At home, his blood pressure hit the roof. He refused to let me call a cardiologist. When it finally reached about 210/120 I insisted and he agreed. I called the doctor and they said to bring him in immediately. The cardiologist examined him and they ran some tests. It was determined that his heart was fine, just elevated blood pressure. His body was pumping blood hard to try to deal with the gaping "hole" in his head. The doctor said it made sense that his blood pressure was elevated because of his wound; in addition, the surgeon had cauterized several arteries. So we went home with a prescription for hypertension.

The following morning we were to begin treating the wound. I got the supplies ready and we washed our hands carefully. Tim pulled off the bandage in front of the bathroom mirror and we gasped.

"Bebe, I'm a monster." No one had prepared us for what we saw. Almost the entire left side of his forehead was a deep open wound. The doctor had told us they were able to leave the final thin layer of skin over the bone. He said without that layer, it is really almost impossible to heal. So we were glad for that layer and we were grateful the cancer had not spread into the bone, but it was like looking inside his head.

As our faces were pressed in close to the large mirror in the bathroom, I glimpsed my own face under the bright lights. "Oh my goodness, Tim! Are you going to love me with all these wrinkles?"

He just looked at me and quipped, "Are you going to love me with a *hole* in my head?"

I don't have a stomach for "blood and guts" but I had to get over that really fast. I tried to reassure him. God helped us both. Tim laid his head on a towel-covered pillow on the floor and I washed, treated, and covered the area. That procedure was repeated several times during the day and before bed. I really don't even know how I was physically able to do what needed to be done, other than

God's enabling power. Tim returned to work several days later and we continued our regimen. Our understanding was that they were going back in later to close the wound, but we soon learned that was not the case. The plastic surgeon explained that it would be at least a year before the skin would be pliable enough to do any stretching and we would have to decide at that time whether it was worth another surgery.

Several weeks following Tim's surgery, his mother suffered a heart attack and was placed in ICU. She remained unconscious and recovery did not appear likely. Bill, my father-in-law, faithfully stood at her bedside or sat in the waiting room until he could be with her again. Tim or his brother would take their dad home after the last visitation, but we learned later from Bill and Peggy's neighbor that she repeatedly saw him backing out of his driveway in the night hours. He was slipping back up to the hospital. Tim said later that he noticed his dad was often in the same clothes as the day before. About a week into this, my father-in-law suffered a massive heart attack in the waiting area and died. They worked for almost an hour but were never able to revive him.

My husband had been going back and forth between work, the hospital, and me. Now he had to help plan a funeral, too. The loss of his Dad was sudden and very difficult. No one was expecting Bill's passing; he hadn't appeared to have any physical problems. Obviously, the years of caring for his wife, the stress of her being in ICU, the fear of losing his precious lifetime mate, and the lack of rest took its toll. We learned later that their funds were surprisingly low and I'm sure he was concerned about the costs for her extended care.

We went home following Bill's funeral to get a few hours rest, but the hospital called before we had even been able to change our clothes saying Tim's mother had regained consciousness and was asking for his father. We immediately left for the hospital and my husband and his brother went in to try to explain what had happened to his dad. We don't know if she ever really understood.

While Tim and Mike were explaining Bill's passing to their mom, two hospital social workers came up to me and my sister-in-law (I was in a wheelchair, unable to walk) and told us the hospital was discharging our mother-in-law. We were informed that we had to make the decision about where to send her immediately. She had just been moved out of ICU into a regular hospital room that morning. I guess Medicare would no longer pick up the charges. I asked them if they knew we had just come back from her husband's funeral. One social worker responded that they did know, but this decision had to be made. She said it was time for her to get off work and she left. However, the other woman was very kind and when Tim and Mike returned, she took all four of us into a room to discuss some things and allow us to have time to take all this in, even though it was also the end of her shift. God had provided another "angel".

The next morning a nurse from hospice came and examined Tim's mom and reviewed her charts. She recognized that Peggy was being kept alive by artificial means and recommended that she be put in final stage hospice. Peggy had been very ill with many complications of diabetes for quite a long time and had requested that she never be kept alive artificially. My father-in-law had responded as any loving husband would when his wife was unresponsive; he called for help. Now, the day after my husband and his brother had buried their father, they had to make a very difficult decision regarding their mother. None of us had any physical or emotional strength left at this point, and every step we took was enabled by the grace of God.

Tim's mom was placed in a beautiful hospice with the most caring nurses who peacefully and lovingly attended to her needs. The next day she slipped back into unconsciousness and never recovered. Her room was large and family members were able to be with her. Two of her grandchildren who live in town spent many hours with their grandmother, sharing their lunch hour to talk to Peggy or playing family videos in the background in case their Mama Peg could hear or might awaken. Someone from the family was always there and if there was a group, we would share stories and laugh and cry, and tell Peggy how much we loved her. A couple of weeks later we had another funeral and another tribute to them as a loving couple, godly parents, and good friends to many.

Chapter Six

A Diagnosis?

At this point, Tim still had a patch on his head, wound cleaning and dressing was not quite as frequent, and we were amazed at how his body was recovering. The wound was shrinking in size and we could see that he was healing. We truly are fearfully and wonderfully made. He is left with a scar, but he is still my handsome knight in shining armor. We have decided not to have any reconstructive surgery on his forehead.

While Tim's mom was still in hospice I had an appointment with another highly recommended endocrinologist. I had tried to see this doctor for about a year, but she was no longer taking new patients. Wanting to help me in some way, a sweet friend had arranged with this doctor to give me her upcoming appointment. This endocrinologist readily recognized that mine was a neurological problem, saying that I presented like her patients who suffered from Multiple Sclerosis. The doctor scheduled an MRI and nerve tests and made arrangements for me to see an experienced neurologist in the Medical Center. She also suggested I wean off the cortisol and reduce my thyroid medication.

Now, following Peggy's passing, my precious husband took me to have the neurological tests performed in the medical center. About a week later, I met with a neurologist who interpreted the results to indicate that I did not have MS, but he thought I presented with symptoms of Myasthenia Gravis. My head bobbed, I had noticeable tremors in my hands and, of course, the odd gait. Some of the tests were inconclusive and he ordered blood work and arranged for me to come back for more testing. However, when I returned he had reviewed everything and decided I possibly had a neurotransmitter deficiency. He felt that somehow the messages from my brain were not reaching my muscles. He called it a "motor problem." He started me on some medication which had an immediate effect but within less than a week, I was worse than before and having numerous side effects. He stopped that medication and wanted me to try another. He said that it would be trial and error before we found something that worked. For several months I had suffered with my eyes staying perpetually dilated. I couldn't stand any kind of light and based on the possible side effects of the new medication (possible blindness was mentioned), I decided to wait before trying out different prescriptions. I went to my eye doctor and she immediately referred me to a neurological ophthalmologist, also suspecting Multiple Sclerosis. After a couple day-long testing sessions with this specialist, I still had no answers. However, she felt almost certain that I did not have MS.

After the one neurologist had mentioned a possible neurotransmitter deficiency I began researching. I found that one could supplement with particular amino acids to build neurotransmitters in the brain. He had mentioned a couple of specific neurotransmitters related to energy and muscles so I started with those. I read a very helpful book by two doctors in San Antonio, Texas, *Heal with Amino Acids and Nutrients.* I went to see my eye doctor again and she asked me what I had been doing because my eyes were no longer dilated. I told her that I had started taking some specific amino acids to build my neurotransmitters. She was very excited about the fact that my eyes were so much better and encouraged me in my pursuit. She mentioned that she had also done some research in this area and that she felt this was the wave of the future for medicine.

I continued my experiment and went back on a follow-up visit with my neurologist. I was doing some better and he acknowledged that, but he did not want me as his patient if I wasn't going to take his suggestions of prescription medicine. So I thanked him for his help and moved on. At a follow-up visit with my endocrinologist, she made arrangements for me to begin physical therapy to help prevent muscle atrophy. I was very limited in what they called "land therapy" so they began me in "water therapy."

I began looking for a doctor who treated with amino acid therapy and hit a wall. However, I found a chiropractor who was willing to help me, connect me with a lab that offered neurotransmitter testing, and at least monitor what I was doing and make suggestions. This seemed to appease my family members who were concerned that I was treating myself. She also was able to help me with chiropractic adjustments. I was aware of improvements, but I still had some serious problems, and I continued to be unable to walk much further than my driveway.

I met with a new internist to determine the efficacy of my supplements. I had previously added a good probiotic and later an enzyme supplement. I wanted to see if they were helping nutrient absorption. His testing determined that my nutrient level was much improved. He also referred me to another neurologist as he felt I still had some serious issues that needed to be addressed. I met with the new neurologist early in December of 2009.

This physician had me perform some slow leg squats. I had described what "used" to happen when I tried to walk but told him that those episodes were not as frequent. However, after only three slow squats while holding on to the counter, my body began to collapse. The doctor held me up to keep me from falling and I began breathing laboriously. My legs were like heavy Jello and I tried to balance on my tiptoes as my muscles drew up in spasms. It turned out that the condition had not improved so much as I had learned my parameters and didn't push myself beyond them (his comments). It was described later by another physician as a "complete physiological depletion of energy." My muscles didn't have what they needed to be muscles. This neurologist again mentioned Myasthenia Gravis. His comment was something like, "I'm pretty sure I know what you have." He ordered very thorough blood work, checking for the condition in several different ways.

When the results came in, the doctor called me at home. He said that the tests did not indicate Myasthenia Gravis, nor did he think that I had a degenerative muscle disease after examining all the previous tests as well. He said that was very encouraging; however, he stated that he did not know how to help me. His words were, "I don't know what to tell you to do. I don't even know what to tell you <u>not</u> to do." He mentioned that there was a muscle specialist in the Houston Medical Center at Baylor that might be able to help me. If I wanted, he would help me get in to see her. The internist agreed and also suggested that he would help me get in to see the muscle specialist. All we knew was that for some reason my neurological system was malfunctioning and keeping my brain from communicating with my muscles. But I was tired. I was tired of doctors, tests, not knowing, waiting, wondering, overwhelming exhaustion, feeling worthless, burdening my husband, everything. I was just tired. There is really not a word to describe the type of overall fatigue I was feeling. We decided to wait a bit before starting over with another doctor.

Chapter Seven

It's just You and me now!

I continued to hold on to the many healing scriptures in the Bible. I read, memorized, spoke and prayed scripture. I told the Lord, "It's just You and me now. I've tried everything I know to try. The doctors don't know what to do for me. Lord, I'm holding on to the truth of Your holy word. I still believe You're going to heal me. You'll have to show me otherwise if that's not Your plan."

His word affirms, *"For I am the LORD who heals you"* (Exodus 15:26 NKJV). Isaiah prophesied, *"Surely He has borne our griefs* [sicknesses] *and carried our sorrows* [pains]*; yet we esteemed Him stricken, smitten by God, and afflicted. But He was wounded for our transgressions, He was bruised for our iniquities; the chastisement for our peace was upon Him and by His stripes we are healed"* (Isaiah 53:4-5 NKJV). The New Testament confirms this in Matthew 8:17 (NKJV), *"that it might be fulfilled which was spoken by Isaiah the prophet, saying: 'He Himself took our infirmities and bore our sicknesses.'"* Another favorite of mine is in Psalm 103; *"Bless the LORD, O my soul; and all that is within me, bless His holy name! Bless the LORD, O my soul, and forget not all His benefits: Who forgives all your iniquities, Who heals all your diseases, Who redeems your life from destruction, Who crowns you with* *lovingkindness and tender mercies, Who satisfies your mouth with good things, so that your youth is renewed like the eagle's*" (verses 1-5 NKJV).

But I had made another decision. It had come to my attention that God desires that we seek Him more than anything else. Had I done that? Or, had I primarily been seeking my healing. Had my healing become my focus? I began to focus on Him, only Him. In my prayer time and throughout the day I would seek His presence. It is very scriptural to bring our needs before the Lord; but I simply changed my focus. I spent most of my days in quiet or vocal praise and worship. I did still tell Him each day that I believed that "by His stripes I have been healed," but my healing was no longer my primary focus.

For several months I had also been focusing on Romans 12:2 (NKJV), *"And do not be conformed to this world, but be transformed by the renewing of your mind, that you may prove what is that good and acceptable and perfect will of God."* With His help, I was endeavoring to line up all my thinking with the word of God.

In searching out everything that had to do with the brain, I came across a teaching by Dr. Caroline Leaf, a neuroscientist, and began to read and implement her book and teachings into my life. In November, 2009, I began to go through some of the exercises Dr. Leaf recommended in her book, *Who Switched Off My Brain.* I learned that the way the brain works totally affirms the Word of God. I learned from her teaching that our thought life and the memories we store either build and heal or release toxins that are destructive to our health. Her book helps the reader learn how to begin to think and store memories based on truth and to retrieve memories that need to be healed.

There is a reason the scriptures tell us not to worry and fret. There is a reason we are to forgive others. There is a reason we are to not judge others, or take offense. Doing things God's way promotes health and peace. Doing things the world's way promotes destruction. *"There is a way that seems right to a man, but in the end it leads to death"* (Proverbs 14:12 NIV).

I learned from watching Dr. Leaf on a television program that toxic thoughts and memories release actual chemicals in our brain that drip poison into our systems, making us sick. When we build healthy thoughts and memories they also release chemicals in our brain called neurotransmitters. Wow! That's exactly what one doctor said I needed.

I have a simple process I seek to follow now. Don't believe or accept something if it doesn't line up with the Word of God. Doesn't He tell us to take every thought captive? *"Casting down arguments and every high thing that exalts itself against the knowledge of God, bringing every thought into captivity to the obedience of Christ"* (2 Corinthians 10:5 NKJV). When you have a hurtful thought or memory, ask yourself, "What does the Word say about this?" As old painful memories come up I ask the Lord to show me the truth about that particular memory and He does. It doesn't mean something hurtful didn't happen, but He gives me a new way of looking at it or understanding the person who hurt me. Then I can file it back in my memory in a non-toxic form. Sometimes it is just a matter of replacing it with a truth from His word or committing the person and the offense into God's hands.

This same process applies to fear and worry. When we really get a concept of God and His love we can experience complete trust in Him and His ways. If we really trust Him, we won't worry or fret. *"Trust in the Lord with all your heart, and lean not on your own understanding; in all your ways acknowledge him, and he will make your paths straight...This will bring health to your body and nourishment to your bones"* (Proverbs 3:5-6, 8 NIV). We may have been taught to worry, but we can unlearn any behavior.

Through all these years of struggle I believed that God is good, that He loved me, that He still had a plan for my life, and that He heals. I had put many scriptures to memory that helped me immeasurably during those sleepless nights filled with anxiety. I listened to preachers who taught on healing. I read and spoke aloud over and over the scriptures on healing. I declared that no matter what happened to me, His Word is true. Even if I never saw my healing here on this earth, God is good and He is faithful to His Word.

My circumstances and my feelings although real are not my truth. His Word is my truth. There is healing in His Word. There is health in His ways. There is hope in His Son. There is life in His Truth. *"Jesus said to him, 'I am the way, and the truth, and the life. No one comes to the Father except through Me'"* (John 14:6 NKJV). In verse 1 He states, *"Do not let your hearts be troubled. Trust in God; trust also in Me"* (NIV). I have learned to trust Him and continue to learn to put that trust into practice.

Sunday night I went to bed an invalid. Monday morning, February 1, 2010, I woke to a new life. Normally, I would stumble from the bed to the bathroom and then struggle to get down the hall often bumping into the walls. This morning I walked tall and strong into the bathroom. As I walked down the hallway with stability and strength I realized something had happened. My legs were not floppy and fragile. My mind was clear; the constant fog had lifted. I was not exhausted; I was strong. I began to cry. I quickly called my husband at work, "Tim, I'm healed! I am whole! I feel like I could run down the street!" His immediate response was, "Oh, Bebe! Don't do that!"

It would be some time before my husband was truly convinced in spite of the amazing change, but I knew. I think he was afraid the symptoms might return. But, it was not just an incredibly good day; I was not just some better. For a week I couldn't stop weeping or praising God; I was filled with overwhelming gratitude. I told everyone in my path, and I'm afraid I still do that to a degree. It's just too good to keep to myself.

Two days after I woke healed I had an appointment with my chiropractor. She saw me walking down the hallway into the examining room. She exclaimed, "You're walking!"

"I'm healed."

She questioned, "No, you just walked in here normally. I've seen you walk; you couldn't even walk in a straight line."

"I know! God has totally healed me," I replied grinning from ear to ear.

She proceeded to ask me several questions. After commenting, "Well, something has happened," she began to examine me to perform the chiropractic adjustments. As her hands moved over my body, she exclaimed, "Bebe, you have muscle tone!"

"I do?"

"In all the time I've been examining you and making adjustments you didn't have muscle tone. You should have muscle atrophy! You don't get muscle tone in two days." She commented that my body was resisting her adjustments, which is a normal response.

Friday of that same week I made a trip to Target, a feat which I had been unable to even attempt for two years. I walked the length of the parking lot, shopped every isle of the grocery department, and having full energy shopped every isle of the remainder of the store. No floppy gait, no dips, no weak spells, only strong steady steps. I then took my purchases to the car, drove home and made several trips carrying everything into the house. I didn't even need to rest! I just proceeded to prepare the evening meal with a really big smile on my face, immeasurable appreciation in my heart, and praise on my lips.

To put this in perspective, most of the time I couldn't even get to the store. On a really good day, I would venture to our small neighborhood grocery and leaning on a grocery cart from the parking lot, I would purchase a few items. Back at the car I would drink a protein drink and proceed to the house. If I was able, I would carry the single small bag of items from the car and once inside make my way to the sofa and lie down for a long rest. That was an exceptionally good day.

One day I miscalculated my abilities and just a couple of items into the shopping I had to lay my upper body across the cart, my head resting on my purse. Insanely, I pushed to the checkout counter determined to purchase the two items, my breathing very labored. Two ladies at the checkout inquired about my condition. One asked me if she should call an ambulance. I insisted that she not do that, just please help me to my car. A young man helped me push my cart to the parking lot as I lay draped across. I gave him the keys to my car and he unlocked it. I literally fell into the car. He looked at me and asked, "Lady, are you going to drive?" I told him I was going to drink a protein drink and wait until I had a little more strength. But I did drive home; I'm sure my angels were assisting!

February, 2010, a full 7 years after my initial jaw injury, God miraculously healed me by His Son's atoning work. I walk completely balanced with a sure steady gait. I can go to any grocery store, hey, even the mall. I can run and play with my grandchildren. I can take long walks with my husband. I can take care of my home again. I can think clearly; I can think rightly. I continue in my pursuit of thinking according to God's Word. I had prayed and asked the Lord to "transform me by the renewing of my mind;" He is transforming me and I am confident that, *"He who has begun a good work in* [me] *will complete it until the day of Jesus Christ"* (Philippians 1:6 NKJV). As the Psalmist declares, *"I hope in Your word"* (Psalm 119:147 NKJV).

Part Two

Learning To Trust

Part Two

Learning to Trust

In one of our conversations regarding my healing I told a neighbor that fret, worry, and fear are indications that we are not trusting God. My neighbor asked me, "How do I get to where you are without going through what you've gone through?" That was a question I had to ponder.

I asked the Lord to lead me in sharing ways of learning to trust Him completely, toward which I am ever striving. As I sat in His presence listening to God's still voice I quickly wrote the ideas that flowed into my thoughts. The following pages include some pathways that the Lord revealed to me in regards to building trust in Him and I am so pleased to be able to share them with you.

Chapter Eight

Relationship

The first essential in trusting the Lord is having a personal relationship with Jesus Christ. I don't want to take for granted that everyone reading this book knows Him personally. Know first that He loves you very much, just as you are. Jesus loves you so much that He left His heavenly kingdom to come to earth as a little baby, and lived a sinless life so that He could become the sacrifice for your sins. He willingly laid down His life for you. He died a cruel death on the cross, but on the third day, He rose from the dead, conquering sin and death, and is now seated at the right hand of the Father.

We all have need of a Savior; *"This righteousness from God comes through faith in Jesus Christ to all who believe. There is no difference, for all have sinned and fall short of the glory of God, and are justified freely by his grace through the redemption that came by Christ Jesus"* (Romans 3:22-24 NIV). There is nothing you can do on your own to earn His forgiveness; it is a gift. Receive the gift, confess that you have need of a Savior, and give Him place in your life as Lord and King. *"If you confess with your mouth, 'Jesus is Lord,' and believe in your heart that God raised him from the dead, you will be saved"* (Romans 10:9 NIV).

Jesus Christ is the only way to a relationship with God the Father. *"Jesus answered, 'I am the way and the truth and the life. No one comes to the Father except through me'"* (John 14:6 NIV). Our relationship with the Father was broken because of sin. Jesus bore our sins when He died on the cross; He became the sacrifice for our sin. *"God made him who had no sin to be sin for us"* (2 Corinthians 5:21 NIV). When we accept Jesus Christ as our Savior and Lord, we accept the gift of His sacrifice. We are then made righteous in the eyes of God and our relationship is restored. *"How great is the love the Father has lavished on us, that we should be called children of God!"* (1 John 3:1 NIV).

Chapter Nine

A Disciplined Mind

Think intentionally. When I am worrying or fretting over something, that thing is continually harassing my mind. It is impossible to simply turn off a thought, but I can replace it with another thought. But with what do I replace it? Replace it with a Biblical truth, something founded on the word of God. Choose a thought. Refuse to allow thoughts to just come and go as they please; think intentionally. Philippians 4:8 (NKJV) counsels, *"whatever is true, whatever is noble, whatever is right, whatever is pure, whatever is lovely, whatever is admirable—if anything is excellent or praiseworthy—think about such things."* That thought concludes in verse 9, *"and the God of peace will be with you."*

Trying not to think about something will just cause you to think about it more. But choosing to think a different way about that issue is a better choice. If possible, take the time to look up a scripture relating to the issue at hand. Many Bibles have a condensed form of a concordance or topical issues for study. There are websites with free accessible information such as commentaries, topical references, and different versions of the Bible. You can access them by scripture reference or topic. You don't even have to download anything. We must choose to *"take captive every thought to make it obedient to Christ"* (2 Corinthians 10:5 NIV), or your thoughts will take you captive.

Change the worry into a prayer. Scripture tells us in Philippians 4:6 (NIV), *"Do not be anxious about anything, but in everything, by prayer and petition, with thanksgiving, present your requests to God. And the peace of God, which transcends all understanding, will guard your hearts and your minds in Christ Jesus."* Take the problem to the Lord for His help and understanding. Decide to pray for the person who has offended you; ask the Lord to bless that person you need to forgive. Ask the Lord to help you see the situation from the other person's perspective. More importantly, ask God to help you see things from His perspective.

Completely change your thoughts by turning them to praise. Think of the many things the Lord has done for you, the times He has come to your aid, the blessings that are in your life. Thank Him for specific things; the list will grow as you focus on what He has done in your life. Start with the simple. For example, "Thank you, Lord, that I have breath. Thank you that I can see. Thank you for running water," etc. There are so many wonderful things that we simply take for granted. We don't think of them because we are so accustomed to having them. It's funny; now I thank Him for the ability to walk through my house, to clean my house, to go to the store. I thank Him for the ability to chew my food as well as my regular thanks for the food on my plate. Choose to take notice and give thanks. Make a list; He has blessed us in so many ways.

Instead of allowing negative thoughts that are so natural to you, "No one cares, I'm so stupid, I can't do anything right, I'm too old, too young, etc." choose to dwell on what God says about you. Ask the Lord to help you see yourself through His eyes. He says you are *"fearfully and wonderfully made"* (Psalm 139:14 NIV). If we are a child of God, He says that we are seated *"in the heavenly places in Christ Jesus"* (see Ephesians 2:6 NKJV). Search the scriptures to see what the Father says about His children. What has Jesus Christ accomplished for you? What does He declare about your life?

Colossians 3:2 (NKJV) admonishes, *"Set your mind on things above, not on things on the earth."* The Greek form of the word "set" means to exercise the mind, to rein in or curb. We need to make a deliberate decision to think according to God's word; however, we do not have to depend on our own strength to do this. God has given us a promise in 2 Timothy 1:7 (NKJV), *"God has not given us a spirit of fear, but of power and of love and of a sound mind."* A sound mind refers to safe thinking or a disciplined mind and the Lord has provided enabling power through the gifts of His Son, Jesus Christ, for us to do just that. There is power in His word. When crippling thoughts come your way, choose the mind that God has given you, a sound mind.

This indeed is a form of exercise. During many long nights without sleep I was gripped with anxiety and fear. I had to battle many anxious thoughts with the truths of God's word, particularly those scriptures I had put to memory. Honestly, until I recognized that this was a spiritual battle, I was in bondage to these thoughts. At times I recognized they were unfounded or ridiculous but I had no control over them, or at least that is what I thought. But the word of God is powerful and as a child of God, His spirit dwells within me. I have the weapons I need to stand against anything the enemy can bring. The Word of God is my offensive weapon to use to tear down any stronghold of the mind.

Chapter Ten

A Strong Defense

Read and memorize scriptures that build your trust.
Rehearse them. Speak them aloud. Choose several
scriptures or even chapters that are very meaningful to you
and ask the Lord to help you put them to memory. It has
never been easy for me to memorize. In school I actually
had to write out important parts of my textbooks. Then, I
would study those notes that I had written and underline
and highlight. It took intensive study time, but I could only
remember what I had first transcribed.

I asked the Lord to help me memorize scriptures. The
first plan of attack was to write out on note cards individual
verses or portions of scripture that I wanted to know by
heart. Then I would study them and read them aloud over
and over. The Lord began to make specific scriptures
become very real to me. The more I read them and spoke
them, the more I loved them.

I read through the Psalms often and as I read Psalm 91
during a particularly difficult time emotionally and
physically, the words simply embraced me and lifted me
up. I decided to put that Psalm to memory. I am so glad I
did. Many anxious, sleepless nights were made more
bearable as I rehearsed that passage over and over in my
mind, taking one verse at a time. A funny thing about

reading scripture and speaking scripture aloud, the more you hear it the more you believe it. That makes Romans 10:17 come alive for me, *"So then faith comes from hearing, and hearing by the word of God"* (NKJV).

There is real power in the Word of God. When I was so weak I could barely speak, I would begin reading a passage aloud. Sometimes it would begin as a whisper and by the end of the chapter I would almost be shouting. I cannot emphasize enough how important the reading of God's word is to your life. Ask the Lord to give you understanding and revelation as you read. *"For the LORD gives wisdom; from His mouth come knowledge and understanding"* (Proverbs 2:6 NKJV).

Seek out a translation that you can understand and read more easily. There are Bibles with several translations parallel to one another for comparison. Many Bibles have study notes in them to help you understand what you are reading. You can compare versions online; one really good site is www.biblegateway.com. Ask friends at church for their input, research online, and then go shopping for a new Bible. If funds are tight, shop a thrift bookstore.

Chapter Eleven

Role Play

Place yourself in Biblical situations. Think about stories in the Bible and imagine yourself in that dilemma. For example, if you are in what appears to be an impossible situation, put yourself there at the Red Sea with the children of Israel. You have the Red Sea in front of you and the Egyptian soldiers bearing down from the rear. You are trapped in human terms, but as children of God, we have kingdom assistance. God made a way for them and He will make a way for you, too.

There are many stories of healing in the Bible. The woman who had been subject to bleeding for twelve years touched the edge of Jesus' garment believing that she would be healed and she was, (see Luke 8:43-44 NKJV). Two blind men followed Jesus. He asked them if they believed He was able to heal them. They did believe, *"Then He touched their eyes and said, 'According to your faith will it be done to you,' and their sight was restored"* (Matthew 9:29 NIV). Jesus opened the deaf man's ears. He spit and touched the man's tongue and he could speak; read about it in Mark 7, verses 31-37.

He calmed the winds and the waves when the disciples were frightened in the storm. He will carry you through the storms in your life. He can speak to your circumstance. He can bring peace to your troubled heart. Keep your focus on Jesus.

As you read your Bible or listen to lessons or sermons, place yourself in those situations and know that God is there for you, too. Run to Him for help and guidance.

Chapter Twelve

Journal

Remember the many ways God has helped you in the past. Write them down. As the Lord prompts you with a memory add it to your list. You will be amazed. We tend to forget the good and dwell on the bad. Be purposeful in remembering all the things God helped you with in the past. If you are a new believer begin a journal to record the special ways God leads you and helps you. God truly cares about your needs and has plans for your future. There are so many examples in my life but as I write, one in particular comes to mind that I would like to share.

My husband and I were in a gospel rock group in the early seventies. We were traveling full time singing at different churches; at this time we were touring the western states. We were at a stately old church in San Francisco and had traveled a long way, gone without sleep and we were hungry. The church was supposed to feed us following the service, but when we finished tearing down and loading equipment the food from the "fellowship" was all but gone, a finger sandwich and a cup of punch. We had not eaten lunch or dinner that day. Six of us were taken to different homes and Tim and I were escorted to an older part of the church building that had previously served as a dormitory for a school. It was now vacant. We stepped into an antiquated elevator with an accordion gate that eerily creaked as it was pulled shut. We passed the dark hallway of each floor until we arrived at the tenth floor. A lonely dangling bulb gave only a glimmer of yellow light as the doors opened to a long darkly lit hallway.

As our escort silently led us down the hall our eyes were drawn into a room from which issued another dim light. As we passed, we saw that the light was coming from an old refrigerator held open by a disheveled looking elderly man, stooped and peering into an empty space. Hoping for the best we both shuddered silently and continued to follow our escort. He stopped in front of a door and proceeded to unlock a long series of deadbolt locks with a large ring of keys. He showed us into a room with a bed, a chair, a lamp table and a bare window. This room was adjoined to a small bathroom housing a rusty metal shower pan surrounded by a clear plastic shower curtain. As the young man left he warned us emphatically not to leave the room for any reason until morning and to keep all the locks, locked. He added, "It's just not safe." After he left, Tim and I just looked at each other in unbelief. We were so tired we decided to just get ready for bed and go to sleep.

I remember praying for our safety and I reminded the Lord we were hungry and asked Him for some really nourishing food. On the road you eat a lot of fast food and churches often provide sandwiches or spaghetti. We shut off the lights and were soon startled by gunshots outside. Evidently there was some kind of gang war going on all night in the street below. We looked out and couldn't actually see anything except what appeared to be some flashes from the firing of the guns. It was a drizzly, cold San Francisco night so we just pulled in tight under the covers, grateful for a warm bed.

In the morning, shots had ceased and a cloudy daylight peaked through the window. Tim took the keys and went out to try to find a newspaper and walk around; he gets restless in small spaces. I locked all the locks behind him and proceeded to the shower. We hadn't had an opportunity to freshen up the day before so I was really looking forward to a hot shower. I turned on the hot water and waited and waited and waited for anything but cold water. Twenty minutes later icy water still showered against the metal pan. I just dropped my head. Tim had been speaking in our services about how God cares about our every need. "Lord Jesus, please may I have some hot water for my shower? I'm hungry, I'm tired, and I'm dirty." I reached my hand back in to check . . . HOT WATER! I jumped in and showered and washed my hair. Tim came back. As I got out and wrapped in a towel I shouted out for him to come quickly. I told him to get in and shower since there was hot water. He did. The water stayed hot until he stepped out of the shower. He reached back in to feel the water and it was icy cold. We both had very hot water for our showers, but when we were done, it was gone.

While getting dressed and still amazed at what happened, the phone rang. We hadn't even noticed we had a phone in the room. I answered it and a lady on the other end said she had been in the service the evening before.

She said the Lord had ministered to her and her husband in a special way.

"My husband and I own a restaurant and Monday is our day off. We are bringing a meal up to the church to serve you and your husband and the other members of your group. Is there anything in particular you are hungry for?"

Oh my goodness! I couldn't believe what I was hearing. "Yes, that would be wonderful. We would appreciate anything, but I have really been hungry for fresh vegetables; we don't get that on the road."

"OK, we'll just bring a variety of things." Then she said they would have it ready downstairs around eleven because they knew we needed to get on the road for our engagement that evening. We got the message to the other group members, finished getting ready and packed our bags, then waited with anticipation.

Carrying our suitcases we walked down the hall (looking to see if our friend was still peering into the refrigerator), and onto the quaint elevator which took us down to the large fellowship hall or kitchen area. These dear, dear people had literally brought their living room so we would feel at home. There were big, cozy chairs and lamps and greenery. Seriously, it looked like a home, not a big empty room. The couple had used a latticework partition and hung artwork as a backdrop for the furniture. Then we looked at a long draped table that was laden with the most delicious assortment of food you can imagine, beautifully and professionally set amid floral arrangements. There were all kinds of fresh vegetables and fruits, assorted breads, meats, seafood. The fresh fruit was served from a large carved watermelon. In February! It was a banquet fit for royalty. Their comment to us was, "Eat to your heart's content."

How the Lord lavished His love upon us through these sacrificing servants still amazes me. We were just a little singing group from Houston, Texas. They wouldn't even allow us to help load everything back onto their trailer because they knew our time was limited. This particular day God showed me first hand, "Bebe, I do care about every need you have. I will take care of you."

Chapter Thirteen

Improved Vision

Ask God to help you see things through His perspective. For years I have prayed this prayer often: Lord, I ask you to help me see with your eyes, to hear with your ears, to understand with your understanding, to speak with your words, and to touch with your touch.

When our boys were growing up we had a very special dog. She was a 100 pound yellow lab who stole our hearts as a puppy and continued to wrap herself into our lives. She was gentle and loving, strong willed, and completely devoted. She worked her way into the house at a very young age and miraculously that non-stop tail never broke anything.

One day I was sitting at the kitchen table looking out of the large bay window where she often watched with her nose pressed against the glass until we returned home. This particular day my eyes focused on the window itself instead of the view. I couldn't believe how filthy the window was, but the Lord used this opportunity to teach me a truth.

He said, "Bebe, do you see how the dirty window clouds the view? Well, in the same way, whatever you see or hear passes through the windows of your mind. Your memories, your experiences, your beliefs and your fears combine to alter what you see or hear. You need for Me to clean your dirty windows."

Apparently He's been trying to teach me this truth for some time now. I think I learned a little bit about seeing others and their actions through this truth, but it is harder sometimes to filter our personal circumstances through His truth. Circumstances can press in and squeeze until we feel trapped and hopeless. But we must learn to filter everything through what He says in His word. His word is our final word. His truth is our filter and our "window cleaner".

Chapter Fourteen

A Heavenly Design

Know that He has a purpose for your life and a good plan to carry out that purpose. *"Your eyes saw my substance, being yet unformed. And in Your book they all were written, the days fashioned for me, when as yet there were none of them"* (Psalm 139:16 NKJV). What? He had a plan for my life even before I was born? Yes.

If you feel you have messed up, know that He knew beforehand and has a plan to bring you out and into His perfect will. If life's circumstances seem to be keeping you from His plan, know that He can work in and through those circumstances to get you where He wants you to be. Rest in Him. Trust Him.

He is good and His love for you as His child is perfect; *"If you, then, though you are evil, know how to give good gifts to your children, how much more will your Father in heaven give good gifts to those who ask him!"* (Matthew 7:11 NKJV). *"For I know the plans I have for you, declares the Lord, plans to prosper you and not to harm you, plans to give you hope and a future"* (Jeremiah 29:11 NKJV).

Ask Him to give you a teachable spirit as you journey with the Lord into His purpose for you. Seek Him and His kingdom first. He will be faithful to finish the job He began in you. Psalm 138:8 declares, *"The LORD will perfect that which concerns me"* (NKJV). The NIV translates the same verse, *"The LORD will fulfill his purpose for me; your love, O LORD, endures forever – do not abandon the works of your hands."*

He is still working out His plans for my life. He is refining my hopes and dreams, but many things that I thought had become unattainable are now back in my focus. Never give up, just ask God to accomplish everything He has planned and designed for your life. He will do it, *"For it is God who works in you to will and to act according to his good purpose"* (Philippians 2:13 NIV). *"May the God of peace...equip you with everything good for doing his will, and may he work in us what is pleasing to him, through Jesus Christ, to whom be glory for ever and ever"* (Hebrews 13:20-21 NIV).

Chapter Fifteen

Be Vigilant

Guard your heart. Be careful where you allow your emotions to go. *"Keep your heart with all diligence, for out of it spring the issues of life"* (Proverbs 4:23 NKJV).

Many times this involves changing our focus. Instead of looking at the circumstance, the offense or the offender, your rights, the lack, the fear, or whatever is in your sights, fix your eyes on Jesus. Hebrews 12 tells us that in running our race of faith we must set aside any hindrance, weight, or distraction that would keep us from running our race with perseverance.

We have the power to choose our responses. Put a smile on your face. Interestingly, often the feeling will follow the action. There are other benefits; you look better and younger when you smile. Fewer muscles are used in a smile than a frown so it takes less effort. Put a smile in your heart. *"In the world you will have tribulation, but be of good cheer, 'I have overcome the world'"* (John 16:33 NKJV). Ask God to help you see the bigger picture knowing that He has a good plan for your life.

I understand there are circumstances that make it difficult to smile, but even if you can't muster a smile on your face ask the Lord to put a smile in your heart.

There are also brain chemical imbalances that require correction. Seek help. Be very careful about what you do. This is an area that I would encourage research into amino acid therapy and neurotransmitters. Some alternative medicine has good science behind it. Check with your physician and carefully research drug contraindications, prescription and OTC.

I am familiar with depression. There have been times in my life when I battled some really heavy emotions that I didn't understand. Many years ago I sought help in the church and found none. But the Lord helped me through His word and through the gentle caring words of my husband. During my illness there were some extremely low times when I felt as if I just could not endure any more, but God was faithful to hold me, to keep me in His safe care, to give me encouragement from His word, and to sustain me by His great power through another day.

Read the Psalms. King David fought some of these emotional battles as well. *"I cry out to the Lord with my voice"* [it's ok to verbalize your feelings to the Lord, He cares]. *"I pour out my complaint before Him; I declare before Him my trouble. When my spirit was overwhelmed within me, then You knew my path"* (Psalm 142:1-3 NKJV). The New Living Translation says, *"I pour out my complaints before him and tell him all my troubles. When I am overwhelmed, you alone know the way I should turn."* Read various versions of different scripture references; this helps provide insight and understanding.

Remember that all problems are temporary. Coming to that understanding was very important in my recovery. Whatever we go through is only for a season and compared to eternity, it's just not that long. No matter what happens to us while we are on this earth, it is temporary. *"Now we see but a poor reflection as in a mirror; then we shall see face to face. Now I know in part; then I shall know fully, even as I am fully known"* (1 Corinthians 13:12 NIV). Imagine looking into the face of Jesus. We will see Him face to face and nothing else will matter.

Chapter Sixteen

Seek Him

Ask the Lord to reveal Himself to you. His presence in your life is mandatory for success, for true happiness, and for total trust. It's when we really know Him and who we are to Him that we can rest in His love and trust His care. Make a study of the names of God. Those names reveal so much about Him, about His character. For example, the name Jehovah Rapha means "the LORD who heals," and Jehovah Jireh translates "the LORD will provide."

Deeper studies reveal even more about the names of God. For example, El Shaddai translates the Almighty God. However, when you study the root words in the Hebrew language you discover that God is an all-powerful sustaining God who gives nourishment, like a mother cares for her young child.

There are free study guides online that you can discover by searching "Hebrew Names of God". One such reference site is located at blueletterbible.org. Click on Study Tools, click on Charts & Outlines, then scroll down to The Names of God. You can even find Names of God in Judaism discussed on Wikipedia.com. There are also many books available on the subject.

Jesus told His disciples, *"He who loves me will be loved by my Father, and I too will love him and show myself to him"* (John 14:21 NIV). He is the Light. Light reveals and darkness hides. His truth is revealed in the Word of God. His Spirit will lead us into all truth, (see John 16:13).

Another thing I like to do on occasion is to go through the alphabet and connect the letter with a descriptive word or noun that tells something about God. This is a great exercise to do while waiting for an appointment in an office, or sitting in your car waiting for a train to pass, etc. I'll give you a few examples: a – Almighty, b – best friend, c – caring, d – dependable, e – everlasting, f – faithful, g – good, h – honorable, i – immovable, j – just, k – kind, l – longsuffering, m - merciful; you get the idea. If you get stuck on a letter, just move on, an idea will probably come to you later. It's not a test, just an exercise. No rules, you can even give as many attributes per letter as you like. But many times as I reflect on the attributes of God in this exercise my heart is drawn into true praise and worship. Try it.

"The LORD also will be a refuge [high tower, defense, secure height] *for the oppressed, a refuge in times of trouble. And those who know Your name will put their trust in You; for You, LORD, have not forsaken those who seek You"* (Psalm 9:9-10 NKJV). Get to know Him. Look for Him. Seek Him. Follow after Him. *"If you seek Him, He will be found by you"* (1 Chronicles 28:9 NKJV).

Chapter Seventeen

Where Is Home?

Abide in Him. Webster's dictionary defines "abide": to rest, or dwell; to continue permanently; to be firm and immovable; to remain, to continue. It means you live there, you don't just visit. He is where you run to, where you go home to. He is your source and sufficiency. He is your center. He is where you rest. The Greek word for abide is "meno" and implies staying in a given place or relationship.

As we know Him more, spending time in His word and in His presence, we grow in relationship with Him and understand that He can be trusted with every aspect of our lives. As we walk with Him, He proves himself over and over and we come to that place of expectancy – a well-placed confidence in His love and care. *"Abide in Me, and I in you. As the branch cannot bear fruit of itself, unless it abides in the vine, neither can you, unless you abide in Me"* (John 15:4 NKJV).

I am nothing without Him, but in Him I am everything He designed me to be.

"Jesus replied, 'If anyone loves me, he will obey my teaching. My Father will love him, and we will come to him and make our home with him'" (John 14:23 NIV). His Holy Spirit dwells in you if you are a believer and follower

of Christ. Abide in His presence. He has made your heart His home. Make your home in Him.

Chapter Eighteen

What Are You Eating?

Choose your words carefully. *"From the fruit of his lips a man is filled with good things as surely as the work of his hands rewards him"* (Proverbs 12:14 NIV). *"He who guards his lips guards his life, but he who speaks rashly will come to ruin"* (Proverbs 13:3 NIV). Yes, we produce fruit by what we say. Words are very powerful. *"From the fruit of his mouth a man's stomach is filled; with the harvest from his lips he is satisfied. The tongue has the power of life and death, and those who love it will eat its fruit"* (Proverbs 18:20-21 NIV).

We are told in the thirtieth chapter of Deuteronomy that we have the word in our mouth and in our heart. We have the choice to obey or disobey His word and in that choice to choose life or death. When we choose and speak His truth we choose life. When we choose and speak the dialogue of this world, we choose death. Choose carefully.

For years I have had to eat very carefully because of my jaw problems, and also regarding nutritional choices. But I have also learned and continue to learn to choose my words very carefully, spoken and unspoken. Choose life.

Chapter Nineteen

A Place of Highest Honor

Honor Him. The word, honor, is defined in Webster's to revere; to respect; to treat with deference and submission; to glorify. To revere is to regard with fear mingled with respect and affection; to venerate. To treat with deference is to yield in opinion, to submit judgment to the opinion or judgment of another. Therefore, to show honor to God is to be in submission to His word in our thoughts and actions.

Honor Him with your time, your resources, your money, your abilities, your words, your actions, your worship, and your focus. He is deserving of all honor. *"Now to the King eternal, immortal, invisible, to God who alone is wise, be honor and glory forever and ever. Amen"* (1 Timothy 1:17 NIV). He deserves the place of highest honor in every aspect of our lives.

Give Him His rightful place in your heart and your life.

Chapter Twenty

What Is He Saying?

Look and listen for Him. Look for Him in your surroundings and your circumstances. Acknowledge Him in the beauty around us. Know that He is at work in our lives, orchestrating events to point us to Him. Listen for His voice in your daily activities as well as in His word. He is present in our lives. He is not "out there somewhere." I can tell you from personal experience that He still speaks to us today. Sometimes He speaks by a prompting in our spirit. Sometimes when we hear a message or read His word, a particular truth will literally jump off the page and into our hearts. Sometimes He speaks in a still, small voice and other times with the voice of thunder.

There have been many times in my life when I have heard the voice of God call my name and speak to me as if in an audible voice. I hear the actual words, but not necessarily through my physical ears.

I will relate one such incident. At one of my lowest points during my illness I lay on the sofa, unable to do much else. I really had no strength even to hold a Bible and read. I didn't care about watching or listening to anything. It was too much effort to speak. I felt totally useless. I felt as if all my dreams had died and I was without purpose or value. Weeping, I called out to God, not with perseverance and faith, not with power and hope, simply with desperation. "God, I can't do anything. I feel so worthless." Those words really expressed that I felt my worth and God's love were tied up in what I was doing. As clearly as if you were sitting in the room and spoke, I heard His gentle voice. "Bebe, don't you know how much I love you? I love you more than you can imagine. If you never do another thing but lie on that sofa I love you just as much as when you were teaching Bible study. My love for you is not based on anything you do, but simply because you are My child." I wept, once again assured of His unending and undeserved love.

Even when we know the truth of His love, we get caught up in the world's viewpoint. So many times we have to earn people's approval. We strive to measure up to our parents' expectations and long for their words of affirmation. We are graded in almost everything we do. But we can't earn His love; it is a gift. We don't work to keep it; it is a gift. We simply accept it. He loved you before you knew him; *"God demonstrates his own love toward us, in that while we were still sinners, Christ died for us"* (Romans 5:8 NKJV). And in Ephesians 2:8-9, Paul affirms, *"by grace you have been saved through faith, and not of yourselves; it is the gift of God, not of works, lest anyone should boast"* (NKJV).

Listen for His voice. He is speaking.

Chapter Twenty-One

Placed Trust

Get rid of other gods. In what do you trust? On whom are you depending? What are you fearful of losing? God is a jealous God. In Hebrew the root word for jealous is zeal, signifying intense desire and passionate commitment. His zeal is for you and He is desirous that you be totally devoted to Him. Why? Because He knows that He is the only one who is really for you. You are only safe in His care. He is the only one that you can truly count on in every situation.

Worry is based in fear; fear is based in a lie. We have fear because we place our trust in someone or something that really is powerless to help us. Many have bought into the world view that certain "things" are what we need for security. When those "things" are threatened, we become fearful.

In what are you believing and trusting? Are you placing your trust in the news or the philosophies of this current world view? Or, is your belief based on God's truth, not just what your Bible teacher said or your mother taught you, but based on your personal belief in the absolute truth of God's word?

In the Psalms David affirms, *"In You, O LORD, I put my trust"* (Psalm 31:1 NKJV). The word "put" indicates an action on my part; I choose to place my trust in God. I have learned from experience that I can not place my trust in self, finances, insurance, doctors, friends and family, abilities, good intentions or actions, a job, the government, church, my health, doctrine, prescription or natural medicines or anything else this earth has to offer. My trust can only be placed in the One who made heaven and earth. And remember He made you and me, too. And then He sent His Son to die in our place.

He sent us His word; His word is truth. He promises to never leave us or forsake us. He promises to shield us and to deliver us if we put our trust in Him. You can put all your marbles in that bag. *"My help comes from the LORD, who made heaven and earth"* (Psalm 121:2 NKJV).

Chapter Twenty-two

Let's Talk

Sit at the feet of Jesus. Spend time with Him; adore Him. Seek Him first instead of your goal even if it is a good one. *"Seek first the kingdom of God and His righteousness, and all these things shall be added to you"* (Matthew 6:33 NKJV). Get acquainted with the Lord. Familiarize yourself with His presence. This is a difficult concept for some because we are so accustomed to "doing" something. Rest in Him and in His peace. Walk into His presence with praise and thanksgiving and with a humble and submissive heart. Read the 23rd Psalm and go with Him to those still waters of rest.

Ask Him to lead your heart as you read His word. Let His Holy Spirit guide you into understanding and revelation of His truth. Tell Him your fears, your desires, the issues of your heart. Listen as He comforts and guides and redirects your heart to the desires of His heart. You will find that what He wants for you matches up with the gifts and abilities He has placed within you. He knows us better than we know ourselves. His ways and desires will lead you to a place of satisfaction, expectancy, joy and peace.

Learn to be comfortable with quiet. This generation is so accustomed to constant input; our attention is directed towards television, computers, cell phones and all the tech paraphernalia. Practice redirecting your attention.

Tip: Turn off the radio for one day, even in the car. Sing praise songs, just talk to the Lord like you would talk to your best friend, and listen with your heart. Instead of fretting anxiously as you wait in traffic or stop for a long train to pass, talk to Jesus. Have a conversation with Him. Think about Him. Tell Him your thoughts and your feelings. Let Him speak to your heart.

Chapter Twenty-Three

I'm Accepted

Be confident in God's love and acceptance. He has done so much to prove His love to us; however, there are times in our lives that we are uncertain that He could love us. Yes, the enemy may place doubts, but most often it is our inability to see ourselves through eyes of love. Proverbs 10:12 tells us, *"love covers all sins"* (NKJV). *"God demonstrates His own love toward us, in that while we were still sinners, Christ died for us"* (Romans 5:8 NKJV). 1 Corinthians 13:8 affirms, *"Love never fails"* (NKJV). 1 John 4:8 states, *"God is love"* and verse 18 reminds us that *"there is no fear in love; but perfect love casts out fear"* (NKJV). We can place confidence in the perfect love of God, not because we are lovely or loveable, but simply because we are His.

Yes, He wants us to walk in love and to obey His commandments. But we cannot earn His love any more than we can earn our salvation. His salvation is a gift, freely given. His love is simply a given. It is who He is. If we are a child of God, we can trust His love even in discipline, reproof and correction. We can trust His love when circumstances seem to overwhelm us. He is faithful and His love is steadfast.

It is good to have friends; it is not good to be isolated. However, as I continued in so many years of physical and emotional difficulty I found myself becoming more and more isolated. I didn't reach out to people very much. I didn't have the energy and I didn't want to burden people who had problems of their own. Tim and I changed churches during this period and we found ourselves without a familiar church "home." We continued to go to church and tithe and I even joined the choir for a time. We tried some of the Sunday school classes, but everything was so difficult. Finally, we were no longer even able to attend.

Many had a hard time understanding what was wrong with me. Well, of course! The doctors couldn't even come to a conclusion. Every doctor treated me for some different ailment, none of which helped. I tried traditional medical doctors and alternative physicians. Some close friends were unable to go the distance. But others prayed for me and continued in prayer. For those prayers and those prayer warriors I am forever grateful. Many called with genuine concern to check on me and inquire about my progress.

Those who ministered effectively offered a non-judgmental acceptance of me whether I was in a pit or standing strong in faith; I didn't have to measure up to their expectations. They prayed with me believing for my healing. They confirmed God's goodness and faithfulness, speaking God's truth over my life. One friend occasionally attended to little things without my asking, such as bringing over a supply of paper towels, some fruit or a meal. They ministered without any expectation of reciprocation. However, at times I felt helpless and alone. Some friends wanted the old Bebe who was fun and upbeat. And honestly, some just had no idea what we were going through. But my loving Lord was always there, always accepting, always encouraging, always understanding, never condemning or accusing

Recognize that God accepts you as you are. If you are in Christ, He works to draw you into His ways and to teach you His truths and to walk with you in an intimate relationship. His ways are gentle and loving like a tender, caring shepherd. If you have not accepted Christ as your Savior, the Heavenly Father offers His Son as atonement for your sins so that you can be one of His own children. Jesus Christ loved you enough, even as you are, to lay down His life for you and to knowingly and willingly suffer the most cruel death and rejection anyone has ever known. For you! You are accepted and loved. Receive His free gift.

I wrote the following verse, "What Kind of Friend is Jesus?" over twenty years ago following a very hurtful experience with a close friend. From that crisis I began to understand the faithfulness of our Lord and Savior and the confidence I could put in Him as my best friend.

What Kind of Friend is Jesus?
by Bebe Willert

He is a friend who will always be there for you.
He will never misunderstand you.
He will always comfort you with words of counsel and
encouragement.
He will always listen.
He will let you express your feelings without placing
judgment.
He will never hold a grudge against you.
He will help you grow in every area of your life.
He will delight in your joy. He will feel pain in your sorrow.
He knows exactly how you feel.
He will impart His knowledge to you as you seek and are
ready to receive it.
He will never put you down.
He will never throw your friendship away.
He wants to spend time with you.
He wants you to do those things that will make your friendship
with Him grow.
He will never fail you even when you fail Him.
He will forgive you when you ask.
He is your best friend in the whole world.

Chapter Twenty-four

Never Alone

Know that He will never leave you or forsake you.
The Lord has given His word, *"Never will I leave you;
never will I forsake you"* (Hebrews 13:5 NIV). He told
Joshua, *"Be strong and courageous. Do not be terrified; do
not be discouraged, for the LORD your God will be with you
wherever you go"* (Joshua 1:9 NIV).

There may be times when you feel like you are all
alone. You are not. The scripture tells us, *"For the LORD
will go before you, and the God of Israel will be your rear
guard"* (Isaiah 52:12 NKJV). The Lord told Joshua, *"Have I
not commanded you? Be strong and of good courage, do
not be afraid, nor be dismayed, for the LORD your God is
with you wherever you go"* (Joshua 1:9 NKJV).

Early in my journey through this illness I sat at my
desk, afraid of what was coming, in so much pain and so
very tired. I said to the Lord, "I can't do this, God." I felt
so inadequate and alone. Suddenly I felt a hand reach into
my chest and lift my heart. Then He just held it there. I
knew that God was saying He would be with me, He would
hold me up, and He would hold on to my heart.

The Psalmist asks in 8:4 (NKJV), *"What is man that You
are mindful of him?"* Being mindful speaks to being
attentive, being watchful. Scripture tells us that God is

thinking about us all the time. *"Many, O LORD my God, are Your wonderful works which You have done; and Your thoughts toward us cannot be recounted to You in order, if I would declare and speak of them, they are more than can be numbered"* (Psalm 40:5 NKJV). Again, in Psalm 139:17-18, *"How precious also are Your thoughts to me, O God! How great is the sum of them! If I should count them, they would be more in number than the sand; when I awake, I am still with You."*

Psalm 121:5 (NKJV) tells us, *"The LORD is your keeper; the LORD is your shade at your right hand. The sun shall not strike you by day, nor the moon by night."* That indicates a 24/7 protector and caretaker. And who is it that is guarding us? *"My help comes from the LORD, who made heaven and earth"* (Psalm 121:2 NKJV). He is able, He is dependable, He is constant. A friend and defender who is always present. When? *"The LORD shall preserve your going out and your coming in from this time forth, and even forevermore"* (Psalm 121:8 NKJV). Walk in security and confidence in the Lord who is always with you.

Chapter Twenty-five

Standing in His Joy

Even after my healing, there were some brief periods of physical difficulty. Nothing like my full-blown illness, yet some of the symptoms cropped up on occasion. After church on a Sunday morning, a gentleman had to help Tim carry me to the car as all my muscles went into total meltdown. One day as extreme weakness hit my legs, I stood in my hallway and quoted scriptures on healing and prayed until the weakness left. There have been times I knew to rebuke the enemy and I would regain my strength immediately. However, any problem that flared did not remain. I truly believe that Satan strategically tried to rob me of my healing.

I do not have all the answers. But I do know that God has healed me. I know that I can trust Him. I feel no fear, just simple trust. I don't always understand what is happening, but I know in whose hands I rest. I believe God is also helping me to address some underlying nutritional deficiencies that may have contributed to my problems before. I will continue to stand on God's word. I will continue to do what I can to live a healthy lifestyle.

During the week before Easter of 2011, I was compelled by the punishment and sore abuse that my Savior bore for me. As I again watched the movie, "The

Passion of the Christ," I was riveted to the screen as the actor portrayed the merciless beating of Christ. *"Let us fix our eyes on Jesus, the author and perfecter* [finisher] *of our faith, who for the joy set before him endured the cross, scorning its shame, and sat down at the right hand of the throne of God"* (Hebrews 12:2 NIV). Joy?...Joy? He considered the forgiveness of my sins through His redemptive power such joy that He was willing to endure the cross. He paid my penalty so that I could walk in relationship with Him and the Father. *"That it might be fulfilled, which was spoken by Isaiah the prophet, saying: 'He Himself took our infirmities and bore our sicknesses'"* (Matthew 8:17 NIV). He bore the brutal beatings so that I could walk in wholeness.

That Wednesday morning I woke with severe burning in my legs after a fitful night. I made a decision and shouted out, "No! God healed me, and I will continue to walk in my healing." The next thirty to forty minutes were spent in spiritual warfare from my bed. I told the enemy that He was not going to rob me of my healing. He had no authority over me. My authority was in the blood of Jesus Christ that was shed for me. Jesus already won the battle; I would simply stand firm in His victory. I quoted scriptures out loud that affirmed my forgiveness, my position in Christ Jesus, my strength, and my healing.

I got out of bed and proceeded to get ready for Bible Study, determined that I would be able to attend. The burning and weakness simply faded away. I walked in complete wholeness for an entire week, until the next Wednesday morning. You would think I could have seen the obvious spiritual warfare to keep me away from Bible

Study that morning, but my mind was clouded by the weakness I was experiencing.

As I struggled to get ready and began to drive to my destination, I was awakened by something in my spirit (kind of like a splash of water in my face). "Wait a minute! I'm healed; Jesus finished it." I refused to submit to the fogginess that was in my brain. I spoke, "I have not been given *a spirit of fear* [or confusion, or timidity, or anxiety] *but of power and of love and of a sound mind"* (2 Timothy 1:7 NKJV). Then I began to praise God, to worship Him and to exalt His name. I began to practice one of my suggestions, going through the alphabet naming attributes of God. The weakness and mental fatigue completely left.

So, I will walk in the truth of His word and use the natural supplemental help that He is showing me along the way as my body progresses toward physical wholeness. It is a journey and we have a faithful Friend who walks with us, teaching us and transforming us along the way.

As I write, I have now been completely symptom free for many months. Through this period of time since my healing I have continued to gain strength and purpose. One doctor expressed her opinion that my long illness had totally depleted my body, "Bebe, it's like you have a hollow leg and we just have to fill it up." When God healed me there was an immediate amazing transformation followed by a period of strengthening and cellular recovery.

I recognize that there is a battle raging as long as we are still on this earth. I may have more encounters with the enemy and his forces, but the victory has already been won and declared. I just have to remember to stand on God's word and everything Jesus Christ accomplished for me. He did it all for you, too. All *"for the joy set before Him."*

Dedication to Tim

At the conclusion of my story I realize so much has been left out. Many things have been excluded for expediency or privacy; however, one more thing must be declared.

I am married to the most wonderful man on this planet. He is not a perfect man, none of us are. God has generously blessed me with a patient, gentle, caring husband who loves me unconditionally. He is such a support and encourager to me. He believes in me. He sees me through eyes of love and he puts my needs before his own. I truly believe God has used him as one way to demonstrate His love for me.

Through our almost forty years of marriage, Tim has helped me to believe in myself and my abilities. I will make most of you women truly envious when I tell you that he is an amazing listener. He's witty and funny and incredibly masculine and strong in character. He can be totally trusted and is a man of integrity. He is a hard worker and a good provider. He is a devoted father and loving grandfather.

I know that in times of difficulty it can be tempting to take out your problems on one another. We have always tried to put each other first and to treat each other with respect. I am so grateful to God that during our long trial we never spoke an unkind word to one another.

To truly demonstrate the kind of man I am married to, I will relate the following story. At one point I had been told by a doctor that I most likely had a degenerative muscle disease. It appeared to be an aggressive form of the disease as my muscle weakness was progressing quickly. Tim had helped me to the car and we were in route to get some dinner. He often would take me out when he got home from work, just to get me out of the house; I'm sure the last thing he wanted to do after a long day's work was to get back in the car and go somewhere, but he did. As we were riding in the car it suddenly struck me that it was very likely that soon Tim would be responsible for my total care, cleaning me, dressing me, etc. I started crying and said, "Tim, I am so sorry. I never dreamed that it would be like this." I expressed my fears of what was to come and how badly I felt that he would have to care for me like that. He simply said, "Bebe, if it comes to that it will be a privilege to care for you."

No words had ever been so comforting and affirming. He didn't have to stop and think about what to say, he just shared his heart.

All through our search for answers Tim believed there had to be help. We spent a great deal of money searching for the right doctor. He had to take me for tests and to doctor appointments and still hold down a full-time job. He had to help with shopping and dinners and housework after very long days at the office. He had to try to encourage and comfort me even on days when I'm sure his strength was expended. But, he was and is always there for me. Thank you, Tim. I love you very much.

113

Thank you, God, for giving me such a wonderful partner in life. I love You, God, with all my heart and mind and strength.

Message to my readers:

I would like to express my appreciation to my readers for coming on this journey with me. May the Lord bless you richly as we continue together on this amazing adventure the Lord has prepared for us.

"Make a joyful shout to the Lord, all you lands! Serve the Lord with gladness; come before His presence with singing. Know that the Lord, He is God; it is He who has made us, and not we ourselves. We are His people and the sheep of His pasture. Enter into His gates with thanksgiving and into His courts with praise. Be thankful to Him, and bless His name. For the Lord is good; His mercy is everlasting, and His truth endures to all generations" (Psalm 100 NKJV).

Healing Scriptures

Exodus 15:26(b) *"For I am the LORD who heals you."*

2 Kings 20:5(b) *"Thus says the LORD, the God of David your father: 'I have heard your prayer, I have seen your tears; surely I will heal you.'"*

Psalm 23:3a *"He restores my soul."*

Psalm 30:2 *"O LORD my God, I cried out to You, and You healed me."*

Psalm 91:9-10 *"Because you have made the LORD, who is my refuge, even the Most High, your dwelling place, no evil shall befall you, nor shall any plague come near your dwelling."*

Psalm 91:14-16 [The Lord says] *"Because he has set his love upon Me, therefore I will deliver him; I will set him on high because he has known My name. He shall call upon Me, and I will answer him. I will be with him in trouble; I will deliver him and honor him. With long life I will satisfy him and show him My salvation."*

Psalm 103:1-5 *"Bless the LORD, O my soul; and all that is within me, bless His holy name! Bless the LORD, O my soul, and forget not all His benefits: Who forgives all your iniquities, Who heals all your diseases, Who redeems your life from destruction, Who crowns you with lovingkindness and tender mercies, Who satisfies your mouth with good things, so that your youth is renewed like the eagle's."*

Psalm 107:20 *"He sent His word and healed them, and delivered them from their destructions."*

Psalm 147:3 *"He heals the brokenhearted and binds up their wounds."*

Proverbs 16:24 *"Pleasant words are like a honeycomb, sweetness to the soul and health to the bones."*

Isaiah 53:5 *"But He was wounded for our transgressions, He was bruised for our iniquities; the chastisement for our peace was upon Him, and by His stripes we are healed."*

Isaiah 58:8 *"Then your light shall break forth like the morning, your healing shall spring forth speedily, and your righteousness shall go before you; the glory of the LORD shall be your rear guard."*

Jeremiah 17:14 *"Heal me, O LORD, and I shall be healed; save me, and I shall be saved, for You are my praise."*

Jeremiah 30:17 *"For I will restore health to you and heal you of your wounds, says the LORD."*

Jeremiah 33:6 *"Behold, I will bring it health and healing; I will heal them and reveal to them the abundance of peace and truth."*

Joel 2:25 *"So I will restore to you the years that the swarming locust has eaten."*

Malachi 4:2 *"But to you who fear My name the Sun of Righteousness shall arise with healing in His wings; and you shall go out and grow fat like stall-fed calves."*

Matthew 4:24 *"Then His fame went throughout all Syria; and they brought to Him all sick people who were afflicted with various diseases and torments, and those who were demon-possessed, epileptics, and paralytics, and He healed them."*

Matthew 8:16-17 *"When evening had come, they brought to Him many who were demon-possessed. And He cast out the spirits with a word, and healed all who were sick, that it might be fulfilled which was spoken by Isaiah the prophet, saying: 'He Himself took our infirmities and bore our sicknesses.'"*

Matthew 10:7-8 [Jesus commissioned His disciples] *"And as you go, preach, saying, 'The kingdom of heaven is at hand.' Heal the sick, cleanse the lepers, raise the dead, cast out demons. Freely you have received, freely give."*

Mark 9:23 *"Jesus said to him, 'If you can believe, all things are possible to him who believes.'"*

John 11:4 [concerning Lazarus] *"When Jesus heard that, He said, 'This sickness is not unto death, but for the glory of God, that the Son of God may be glorified through it.'"*

Acts 9:34 *"And Peter said to him, 'Aeneas, Jesus the Christ heals you. Arise and make your bed.' Then he arose immediately."*

James 5:15 *"And the prayer of faith will save the sick, and the Lord will raise him up."*

3 John 2 *"Beloved, I pray that you may prosper in all things and be in health, just as your soul prospers."*

(All Healing Scriptures listed are from the NKJV)

About the Author

Bebe is married to her lifetime sweetheart, Tim, and they have two married sons, Andy and Matt. Two precious daughters-in-law, Erin and April, complete their family and God has now blessed them with grandchildren who are indescribable. However, if you ask, Bebe will be happy to try.

Bebe and Tim began their married years together singing and touring with the JG's, Jesus Generation, a gospel rock band, in the early 70's. She and her husband also enjoyed many years of music ministry in the church. Her love for music continues and she enjoys sharing songs she has written.

With a degree in elementary special education, Bebe has enjoyed an eclectic variety of work experiences. She also served as principle speaker and mentor for MOPS, Mothers of Preschoolers, at a local church for four years. She is passionate about sharing God's relevant truths and unconditional love whether speaking to ladies' groups, church gatherings, or teaching Bible studies.

Bebe is also zealous about prayer. She serves as Prayer Ministry Coordinator for Merry Ministries in Sugar Land, Texas. God has gifted her to aptly apply scripture and to write prayers focusing on the sufficiency of God, no matter the need.

Her utmost desire is to share her story of God's steadfast faithfulness and the undefeatable hope He offers. You can contact Bebe for speaking engagements or book orders through www.bebewillert.com.

With Morning Came Healing

To Kelly

Debe Willert

Psalm 30:2

With Morning Came Healing

A Story of Persevering in Hope

Bebe Willert